The Adventures of
Super Saiyajin Mike

Written by: Michael Sebastian Romero

Illustrated by: Eri Lizbeth & Wendy Silva

The Adventures of Super Saiyajin Mike

Published by FOER
Long Beach, California
First edition, 2026
ISBN: 979-8-9957079-9-8

Printed in the United States of America

For my Everlasting Dragon — you are the reason I build, the reason I dream out loud, and the reason every adventure in this book matters. The world will know Super Saiyajin Mike. But you will always know the real story.

About the Author
Michael Sebastian Romero is a Grammy-nominated,
multi-platinum and diamond certified music engineer and
producer from California. He has spent his career building sounds,
chasing dreams, and learning that every hard day adds one more
layer to who you are. The Adventures of Super Saiyajin Mike is his
first book — but if you know Mike, it won't be his last.

Meet
Mike!

This is Mike.
He loves one thing more than anything in the whole wide world — music. If you listened close enough, you could hear a joyful beat booming from his heart.

Even when Mike was very little, music found him first. He banged on pots and pans in the kitchen. He played every instrument he could find at church.

Mike played the clarinet, the saxophone, the bass, and the drums. But when he got older, he found something new — a pair of turntables. He walked to record shops and dug through boxes of music for hours, looking for new sounds and rhythms.

In college, Mike played music everywhere he could. One night, someone important was listening. That one night turned into two whole years on the biggest stages he had ever seen.

But not everything went the way Mike planned. Sometimes life puts walls in front of you that you didn't build. Mike had to leave school, and it hurt. But he didn't stop. He found a new school — one that taught him how to build music with his hands and his ears.

Mike got a job at one of the most famous recording studios in the world — The Record Plant. The work was hard. Really hard. But the people there became family. They all loved the same thing he did.

And for the first time, it felt like home. Not just any home — the kind where you walk in and everything inside you says: "This is where I'm supposed to be."

The best part wasn't just the music. It was making it with someone else. Late nights, headphones on, figuring out the next sound together. That's where the magic lived.

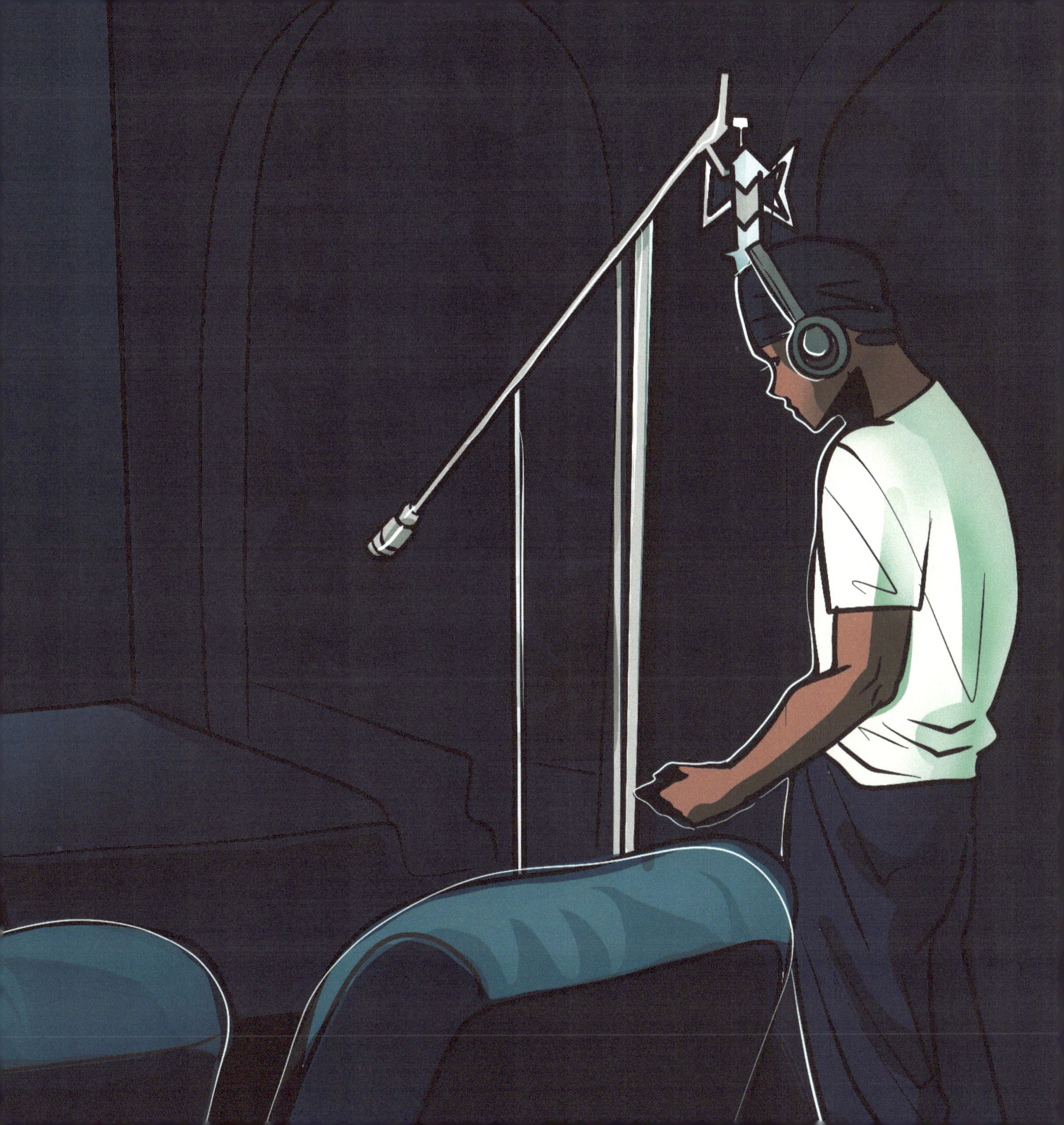

Some days it felt like nothing was moving. Mike wanted to quit. But he didn't. He kept going — one more day, one more try, one more round.

Not every day was a win. But he showed up for all of them. There are no losses. Only lessons.

And then one night, everything they built came together. The sound was right. The feeling was right. No one had to say it — they just looked at each other and smiled.

After years of hard work, Mike got to make music with some of the biggest artists in the world.
JAMES DEAN DEATH CULT

Some nights, Mike loved music so much he couldn't let go — not even in his sleep. He fell asleep holding his keyboard like a teddy bear, still hearing melodies in his dreams.

Before he knew it, Mike learned how to fly. Not with wings
— but with everything he had built inside himself.
"Fly high, never low. When the call comes, trust and go.
Never sell your soul. Talk to God — He will keep you whole."

Mike learned something important: you don't just grow up — you grow layers. Every skill, every gift, every hard day adds one more layer to who you are.

But in between all the adventures, there are quiet moments too. The people cheering for you along the way — that's what makes it all worth it.

Now it's your turn.

Every adventure starts with a single step — a sound you can't stop hearing, a dream you can't stop chasing, a thing you love so much you'd hold it in your sleep.

What's yours?

There are no losses, only lessons.

The Adventures of Super Saiyajin Mike is the
true story of a dreamer who turned late nights,
hard days, and a love for music into something
bigger than he ever imagined. A story about
growing layers — not just growing up.